Dorothea Mackellar's

My Country

a centenary celebration
1908 – 2008

TO PENNY, ANTHONY AND ANNA

PETER LUCK

A familiar face on the Australian media landscape for 40 years, television journalist and photographer
Peter Luck is a renowned chronicler of Australiana. He has presented and produced most of Australia's major
current affairs programs, including *This Day Tonight*, *Four Corners*, *Sunday* and *Today Tonight*. A Churchill Fellow and
Logie winner, he was also producer/presenter of some of Australia's most ambitious and best loved television series
including *This Fabulous Century*, *Bicentennial Minutes … A Time to Remember* and *The Australians*, as well as the
opening night of SBS, and numerous other television specials including *Where Are They Now?* He is the author
of ten books, and his photographic works are included in the collections of the National Portrait Gallery,
the National Library of Australia and the State Library of New South Wales.

Dorothea Mackellar's
My Country
a centenary celebration
1908 – 2008

PHOTOGRAPHED BY PETER LUCK

Social butterfly: Dorothea Mackellar, aged 33, dressed as one of the Three Graces for Mrs T. H. Kelly's Italian Red Cross Day tableau, 20 June 1918. (Reproduced courtesy State Library of NSW)

Dorothea and her country

The poet and author Dorothea Mackellar was just a teenager when she wrote *My Country* — a simple, evocative poem that has become Australia's unofficial spoken national anthem.

Over the years millions of Australian schoolkids have recited the words 'I love a sunburnt country', and the phrase 'wide brown land' is as familiar as Donald Horne's 'the Lucky Country'.

My Country was first published in 1908 — exactly a hundred years ago as I write this — in the English magazine *The Spectator*. Then, Dorothea still called her poem *Core of My Heart*.

As with other anthems, there is a verse that's rarely recited. The first stanza is a description of the British landscape — in stark contrast to the country yearned for by a patriotic young dreamer, beguiled by the character of the Australian bush.

> The love of field and coppice,
> Of green and shaded lanes,
> Of ordered woods and gardens
> Is running in your veins,
> Strong love of grey-blue distance,
> Brown streams and soft dim skies —
> I know but cannot share it,
> My love is otherwise.

No, Dorothea did not share that love for the green and scepter'd isle that was England. She loved a land of sweeping plains, of ragged mountain ranges, of droughts and flooding rains — a wilful, lavish land whose inhabitants were mesmerised by both its beauty and its terror.

It seems paradoxical that Australia's most famous poem, set far from the city, was penned by a delicate, young socialite, the daughter of a wealthy doctor and politician who owned homes in Sydney's most affluent suburbs as well as a string of country properties. *My Country* is at times tough, even sardonic; to me it feels as though it might have been written by A. B. 'Banjo' Paterson, a flinty bush horseman and war correspondent, or by Henry Lawson, a hardened, world-weary journo with a drinking problem.

But, rather, it was the aristocratic, well-educated Dorothea Mackellar who so perfectly captured the ambivalence of the Australian ecosystem and the capriciousness of its climate. Perhaps only P. J. Hartigan (John O'Brien), in his famous comic poem *Said Hanrahan*, expressed so well those extraordinary vicissitudes of the man on the land: first crushed by the drought, then almost drowned by floods — floods that in turn cause the grass to grow so high that the men and women of the bush are faced with the new threat of bushfires!

Many have simply assumed that Dorothea wrote the poem during a bout of homesickness, but the cognoscenti refer to a letter she wrote decades later to her fellow poet and author, Ian Mudie, which implies that she created the work more in a mood of anger, or at least annoyance, about 'the anti-Australianism of many Australians we knew'. She was reportedly particularly irritated by the landed colonial gentry who had made their fortunes in the antipodes, yet whose primary allegiances still lay with what they called 'The Mother Country' in the northern hemisphere.

Sister Adrienne Howley, the nurse who cared for the aged Dorothea during the last 11 years of her life, wrote a memoir called *My Heart, My Country*. In it she recounts how the teenager, when she left for England with her parents in 1903, was told by some:

Dorothea's modest little handwritten notebook of collected poems, which she began assembling at the age of 22, is now one of the treasures in the collection of the Mitchell Library of New South Wales. (Reproduced courtesy State Library of NSW)

'How lucky you are to be going home'.
'I'm not going home, I'm leaving home', Dorothea replied.
'Don't you feel, when you come back, that the Heads [of Sydney Harbour] are closing behind you like prison gates?'.
Dorothea had insisted, 'The Heads are the gates of my home … and I return through them with joy'.

In 1967, only months before Dorothea died, she was interviewed for the ABC TV program *This Day Tonight* by a teenager, Christine Roberts, who had set *My Country* to music. Dorothea was 82 and bed-ridden but still perfectly lucid.

Roberts: Did you have any special reason for writing the poem?

Mackellar: Not really a special reason — but a friend of mine was speaking to me about England — we had both recently come back from England and she was talking about Australia and what it didn't have compared with England. And I began talking about what it did have that England hadn't, that you couldn't expect an old country to have. Well, of course, there are lots of wonderful things, especially in the older parts. But they are not the same. And, of course, the people who came here at first — and I'm not blaming them for it — but it was so different from anything they'd known. They didn't understand.

Certainly, Mackellar showed on many occasions during her life that she had forthright opinions and could be feisty, and, whatever the motivation for her best known poem, it was sustained and determined — she constructed the 48-line work over a period of four or five years.

After its debut in *The Spectator*, the poem was published again on 21 October 1908 in the *Sydney Morning Mail* and later featured in other Australian newspapers and journals. It was still entitled *Core of My Heart* when it was published on the Red Page of *The Bulletin* on 27 April 1911; a review of the poem said, 'its freshness and sincerity put the author in the front rank of those who are now writing verse in Australia'. What made Dorothea change, or agree to change, the original, somewhat awkward and pretentious Edwardian title

Core of My Heart, to the pristine *My Country* is not clear, but it was for the better. Over the years the poem has appeared in more than 20 anthologies, inspired suites of paintings by Australian artists such as J. J. Hilder, been set to music, become a stage musical and featured in films, on television and even in commercials.

Dorothea, or rather, Isobel Marion Dorothea Mackellar was born at her family home 'Dunara' at Point Piper, overlooking Rose Bay on Sydney Harbour, on 1 July 1885, the only daughter of physician Sir Charles Kinnaird Mackellar and his wife Marion. Mackellar, the son of Scots who had migrated to Australia in the 1830s, was for 40 years a member of the Legislative Council of New South Wales and in 1903 became a Senator in the new Federal Government. He was knighted in 1912, and in 1916 was made a Knight Commander of St Michael and St George (KCMG). Sir Thomas Buckland (1848–1947), Dorothea's grandfather on her mother's side, was equally illustrious — a noted businessman and philanthropist whose many public gifts even included the purchase of a bomber for the RAAF in 1940.

Dorothea's early life was luxurious. The impressive family home stood on 5 acres of land in a suburb where houses are sold today for more than $30 million; it included a large garden, part cultivated, part natural bush. The Mackellar family also owned a number of spreads in the north-east of New South Wales, including 'Torryburn' on the Allyn River near Maitland, and 'Kurrumbede' and 'The Rampadells' in the Gunnedah area — properties where Dorothea spent holidays and became a competent horsewoman, riding side-saddle as befitted a woman of her class. She was also a strong swimmer, and was taught to sail and fish.

In her early years she was part of a sort of private kindergarten that included the children of the New South Wales Governor, Lord Carrington; she was

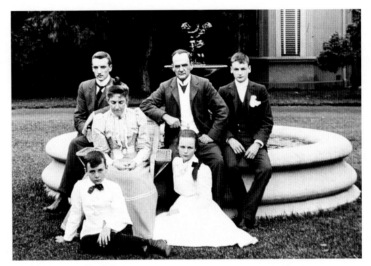

The Mackellar family at 'Dunara': Dr Charles Mackellar; his wife, Marion; three sons, Eric, Malcolm and Keith; and daughter, Dorothea. (Reproduced courtesy The Dorothea Mackellar Estate)

taught by governesses and later by special tutors in fine art, languages and even fencing. Like many other well-heeled colonials, Dorothea received the classic finishing touch to her education, travelling a number of times to Europe with her parents, for whom she became a translator. Dorothea was fluent in German, Spanish, French and Italian. After enrolling at the University of Sydney she accompanied her parents when they had to spend time in England for business and personal reasons and moved between the *beau monde* of Sydney and London with ease. Although she had been born with a silver spoon in her mouth — and no doubt one with all the correct hallmarks — she had an outgoing personality and a keen sense of humour.

Dorothea was beautiful, intelligent, witty and wealthy — but unlucky in love.
(Reproduced courtesy The Dorothea Mackellar Estate)

Dorothea was a romantic. She and her lifelong friend Ruth Bedford by all accounts had a theatrical sense of drama and fantasy, and in secluded bush settings would act out stories and characters they had created together. The titles of her books of verse give a hint of what was going on her imagination: *The Witchmaid* (1914), *Dreamharbour* (1923) and *Fancy Dress* (1926).

Indeed, Dorothea was perhaps the classic 'hopeless romantic', which becomes more evident later in maudlin works such as *Sorrow* and *Riding Rhyme* ('Ride, ride, while the dawn is cool, I was angry and he was a fool'). She was twice engaged but never married and her private life seems to have been permanently tinged with sadness. Keith, one of her three brothers, and much cherished, volunteered for service in the Boer war in South Africa and was killed when only 19. Dorothea never got over this loss.

Young Dorothea's first love affair, an unrequited infatuation with an older married man, a friend of her father's, was a doomed relationship. In 1908 she was briefly engaged to a young Australian. However, that came to an end because of what she considered her fiancé's over-protectiveness, after he objected to her acceptance of a single invitation to the Governor's ball in honour of the visit by the American Navy ('The Great White Fleet'). According to Adrienne Howley, she told him, 'If you have so little trust in me that you expect I will fall into the arms of the first sailor who makes advances then you little know me', and returned his ring.

Dorothea became engaged again in London just before the First World War — this time to Patrick Chalmers, a wealthy businessman and poet, to whom she had written a fan letter. But this affair would also end in heartbreak.

Given her poetic view of most things, one should perhaps regard latter-day accounts of Dorothea's love life with a hint of scepticism — but here is a precis. Just days before her scheduled departure for Australia, Patrick proposed that they marry. She was delighted, but hesitated. It was decided she would return home to tell her parents of the arrangements and generally observe the protocols of the day. According to Adrienne Howley, Dorothea felt 'a temporary parting would be a test of Patrick's love for her'. Back in Australia she wrote to her fiancé to tell him of her parents' approval. But she received no reply.

After the war was over Dorothea journeyed to England again. She had concluded that her lover had lost interest or might even be dead. Dorothea discovered Chalmers was alive; he had not received her letter, assumed that she had changed her mind and married another woman. It was all very sad.

Dorothea, however, was still just an optimistic 17 year old when her very first work was published; the poem *An Old Song* was accepted by the prestigious American magazine *Harper's* along with other short pieces. Her poems also appeared in *The Bulletin* and other quality journals. Her first collection of verse, *The Closed Door*, which included the newly titled *My Country*, was published on 11 May 1911. Mackellar also wrote two light novels — *The Little Blue Devil* and *Two's Company* — in collaboration with Ruth Bedford; another of Dorothea's books, *Outlaw's Luck*, was published by Mills & Boon in 1913.

She was barely 18 when she began dreaming up her little masterpiece *Core of My Heart* in England. After several drafts, she completed the poem back in Sydney. The family now lived in another splendid house, 'Rosemont', in Woollahra, while Dorothea occupied the apartments above her father's medical practice in Buckland Chambers, Liverpool Street, across the road from Sydney's ANZAC Memorial in Hyde Park.

The poem itself is a model of clarity, but its background something of an enigma — there is still conjecture about exactly what inspired the work and, indeed, about the precise words. For instance, the original version for publication reads:

And orchid-laden tree ferns
Smother the crimson soil.

Mackellar later changed it to

And orchids deck the tree tops,
And ferns the warm dark soil.

Interestingly, though, in the only recording made of Dorothea herself reading the poem, in 1958, she uses a third variation:

And orchids deck the tree tops
And ferns the crimson soil.

Overall, these subtle changes mean little — except to indicate the loving care that obviously went into the meticulously crafted piece. Dorothea tinkered incessantly with the poem and the question lingers … exactly when, where and why did the Muse strike Ms Mackellar?

Among the catalysts suggested are, firstly, that notion of the lonely and moody young woman in the unfamiliar and gloomy English landscape — covered as it is in a patina of mouldering history. Her homeland, on the other hand, was entering the bright new twentieth century in a blaze of sunlight, celebrating the official birth of the Australian nation — Federation — on 1 January 1901.

The gardens are now lushly landscaped at Torryburn Stud, near Maitland, but around 1900 'Torryburn' was in the grip of a terrible drought. The breaking of the drought is thought to have inspired a teenage Dorothea to write her famous poem. (Reproduced courtesy Torryburn Stud)

Perhaps, the dichotomy between claustrophobic England and wide open Australia had been working on Dorothea's psyche from her earliest awakenings. She made the first of many trips to England at the age of just two!

No doubt, too, there were certain critical events that reinforced her dramatic notions. In 1900, 15-year-old Dorothea was at 'Torryburn' when the drought broke. According to the *Newcastle Herald*, Dorothea recalled in an interview in 1964:

> … 'there had been a drought, then rain, and we all danced in the flooding rain … I was on my parents' property out of Maitland ['Torryburn'] and, after the rain I was on the verandah writing a long letter to a friend in England. The paddock was cracked from the drought, a dark colour. As I wrote the letter, the land to the horizon became green. After the poem was published, people wrote to me and said they understood exactly what I meant, but they did not have the words for it. I saw it happen, literally'.

Despite its general popularity right from the start, *My Country* has been treated warily by the literary world. Some have even argued it is little more than doggerel. It has been described by one critic as a 'passionate, unsubtle lyric' and as lacking 'the intellectual quality of the best modern poetry'.

Certainly, it is not Shakespeare or Milton; however, to me, no other Australian verse, except for the observation of the drought by the likes of W. H. Ogilvie, Judith Wright and Geoffrey Dutton, evokes the landscape and moods of the country so succinctly. As for Dorothea's own opinion of the poem, she told her biographer Adrienne Howley, 'all I can say of *My Country* is that I wrote it with sincerity'.

Mackellar's creative output had begun to decline after her father's death in 1926 (her mother would die in 1933) but she was still published in quality journals in the 1930s, and she remained on the cultural scene. After the First World War, Mackellar had helped to establish a Zonta Club in Sydney, an organisation begun in America with the stated aim 'to generally advance the status of women'. Mackellar became honorary treasurer of the Bush Book Club of New South Wales and at the beginning of the 1930s she also helped with the establishment of the Sydney Publishers, Editors and Novelists Club (PEN).

Dorothea owned two houses, one at Church Point, Pittwater, and a town house called 'Cintra' on Darling Point Road. In later life she was often in poor health ('a not particularly robust dormouse', the *Australian Dictionary of Biography* says of her), and she spent more than ten years as a patient in Helenie Hospital, Randwick.

Against the advice of her doctors she insisted on returning to 'Cintra', where she suffered a serious fall after she got out of bed to watch birds in her garden. In the 1968 New Year Honours list she was awarded the Order of the British Empire (OBE) for her contribution to Australian literature. Just two weeks later, on 14 January, she died in her sleep in the Scottish Hospital in Paddington. She had outlived all her family and died a wealthy but essentially lonely old woman.

Her funeral service was held at St Mark's Darling Point in Sydney, a church better known for its society weddings. The service included a reading of one of Dorothea's poems, which, to the surprise of most people there, was not *My Country* but a similar salute to her homeland called *Colour*. She once said about *Colour*, 'You know, I think that was as close as I ever came to writing poetry'.

Great saffron sunset clouds, and larkspur mountains,
And fenceless miles of plain,
And hillsides golden-green in that unearthly,
Clear shining after rain.

Not many Australians would agree that *Colour* eclipses *My Country*. It was, after all, *My Country* that had foretold her destiny — we had known for 50 years before her death to what brown country her homing thoughts would fly.

Peter Luck
2008

My Country

by Dorothea Mackellar

There have been many variations of *My Country* published during the past hundred years, but this version reproduces the words read by Dorothea herself in 1958 in the only recording she ever made of her poem.

The love of field and coppice,
Of green and shaded lanes,
Of ordered woods and gardens
Is running in your veins,
Strong love of grey-blue distance,
Brown streams and soft, dim skies—
I know but cannot share it,
My love is otherwise.

I love a sunburnt country,

A land of sweeping plains,

Of ragged mountain ranges,

Of droughts and flooding rains.

I love her far horizons,

I love her jewel-sea,

Her beauty and her terror —

The wide brown land for me!

The tragic ringbarked forests

Stark white beneath the moon,

The sapphire-misted mountains,

The hot gold hush of noon,

Green tangle of the brushes,

Where lithe lianas coil

And orchids deck the tree tops

And ferns the crimson soil.

Core of my heart, my country!

Her pitiless blue sky,

When sick at heart around us,

We see the cattle die —

But then the grey clouds gather,

And we can bless again

The drumming of an army,

The steady soaking rain.

Core of my heart, my country!

Land of the Rainbow gold,

For flood and fire and famine,

She pays us back threefold —

Over the thirsty paddocks,

Watch, after many days,

The filmy veil of greenness

That thickens as we gaze ...

An opal-hearted country,

A wilful lavish land —

All you who have not loved her,

You will not understand —

Though earth holds many splendours,

Wherever I may die,

I know to what brown country

My homing thoughts will fly.

Photographic locations

Thank you

This homage to Dorothea Mackellar and our beloved country owes its existence to many remarkable women. First, my thanks to Caroline Mackaness, General Manager of the properties of the Historic Houses Trust of New South Wales and a driving force behind the Museum of Sydney, and Anne Sullivan, another longtime friend and Dorothea devotee, who kept the faith; Anne helped me research the project and both she and Caroline urged me on when I had given up hope of ever bringing a book like this to fruition. Poetry, along with photo essays, are rare flowers in the publishing garden and need tender care and encouragement to survive, let alone flourish. I was lucky. I was introduced by another dear friend, colleague and author, Eileen Naseby, to the Publishing Director of Murdoch Books, Kay Scarlett, who lifted my spirits with her passion and enthusiasm for this book which she and her team have made so beautiful. She loved the concept from the first moment and imbued me with her energy and drive. The talented team who worked on this project include Murdoch Books' Diana Hill, Editorial Coordinator Kate Fitzgerald, Senior Production Controller Nikla Martin and Publishing Coordinator Jacqui Smith. My gratitude goes to the late Sister Adrienne Howley for her memoir *My Heart, My Country* which tells us so much about the woman she nursed for the last 11 years of her life; to local historian, Val Anderson, for her labour of love, *The Dorothea Mackellar My Country Paterson Valley Connection*, an invaluable reference source; to Barbara Guest and the Dorothea Mackellar Memorial Society for their help and for their effort in creating Australia's largest poetry competition which now attracts more than 15,000 entries each year; to Leigh Priestley of Torryburn Stud for enthusiastic assistance; to Elizabeth Ellis, the New South Wales Assistant State Librarian and Rosemary Moon, the Library's Events and Exhibitions Manager, for their encouragement; to photographer Tonia Arapovic, who helped me with the original digital scans of awkward photographic formats that required the making of special mattes for scanners and other technical niceties; to Pippa Masson of the Curtis Brown Agency for her patience during our protracted liaison to make this project work; to the administrators of the Estate of Dorothea Mackellar who proudly carry the torch for their revered ancestor and handle the legend with great care and respect. And of course, many, many thanks to my family, to my wife, Penny, and daughter, Anna, for their forbearance, and my son, Anthony, his wife Sam and her mother, Eve, for all their support and enthusiasm when the dream of creating a centenary tribute seemed just that — a dream.

First published in 2008 by Pier 9,
an imprint of Murdoch Books Pty Limited
Reprinted in 2009

Murdoch Books Australia
Pier 8/9, 23 Hickson Road
Millers Point NSW 2000
Phone: +61 (0) 2 8220 2000
Fax: +61 (0) 2 8220 2558
www.murdochbooks.com.au

Murdoch Books UK Limited
Erico House, 6th Floor
93–99 Upper Richmond Road
Putney, London SW15 2TG
Phone: +44 (0) 20 8785 5995
Fax: +44 (0) 20 8785 5985
www.murdochbooks.co.uk

Chief Executive: Juliet Rogers
Publishing Director: Kay Scarlett

Editor: Kate Fitzgerald
Concept and Design: Jay Ryves
Picture Researcher: Jacqui Smith
Production: Nikla Martin

National Library of Australia Cataloguing-in-Publication Data
Luck, Peter
My Country/
Dorothea Mackellar / Peter Luck
Sydney: Murdoch Books, 2008.
9781741962819 (hbk.)
Bibliography
A821.4

A catalogue record for this book is available from the British Library.

Printed by 1010 Printing International Limited. PRINTED IN CHINA.